The Population of Chicago

Analyzing Data

Anna McDougal

COMPUTER SCIENCE For the REAL World™

Rosen Classroom™

Published in 2018 by The Rosen Publishing Group, Inc.
29 East 21st Street, New York, NY 10010

Book Design: Jennifer Ryder-Talbot
Editor: Caitie McAneney

Library of Congress Cataloging-in-Publication Data

Names: McDougal, Anna.
Title: The population of Chicago: analyzing data / Anna McDougal.
Description: New York : Rosen Classroom, 2018. | Series: Computer Kids: Powered by
Computational Thinking | Includes glossary and index.
Identifiers: LCCN ISBN 9781508137665 (pbk.) | ISBN 9781538324349 (library bound) |
ISBN 9781508138068 (6 pack) | ISBN 9781538352717 (ebook)
Subjects: LCSH: Chicago (Ill.)--Juvenile literature.
Classification: LCC F548.33 M33 2018 | DDC 977.3'11--dc23

Manufactured in the United States of America

CPSIA Compliance Information: Batch #WS18RC: For Further Information contact Rosen Publishing, New York, New York at 1-800-237-9932

Table of Contents

Population data **determines** the number of seats each state has in the U.S. House of Representatives.

What Is Population?

What can data tell you about your city or town? Data can tell you about the history of a place, as well as its population and popular **industries**. The government collects data on the people and businesses that exist in a place. People analyze, or look at, this data to learn how the place is changing over time.

Population data tells you the number of people who live in a certain place. It's collected through a census. A census is an official count of a population, which also records personal details about people, such as their **ethnicity** and age. The U.S. Census Bureau takes a major census every 10 years.

Urban Populations

Places are usually **classified** as urban or rural. The difference between them has to do with population. Urban areas have populations of 50,000 or more people. Rural areas have populations of fewer than 50,000 people. The area just outside of a city is usually called suburban.

How are urban and rural places different for the people who live there? Urban places generally have many apartments and buildings that are close together. More people have to fit into the space. In rural places, there is space between houses—sometimes miles! Suburban places are in the middle. There are usually many houses, which are usually separated.

Cities are often home to tall buildings called skyscrapers.

Chicago was home to former president and first lady, Barack and Michelle Obama.

The City of Chicago

Some of the biggest cities in the United States are New York City, Los Angeles, Chicago, and Houston. They have the largest populations. Because of that, many businesses and jobs are available. Cities often have **diverse** populations.

Over time, the population of a city changes. Some city populations grow, while others shrink. Chicago is one city that has an ever-changing population. You can look at data from the city of Chicago to learn about how it has changed from year to year, and decade to decade. This can help you learn more about factors that are linked to population, such as business growth and cost of living.

Chicago History

To learn more about Chicago, you can collect information about its history. Chicago was founded in the 1830s in the state of Illinois. This is in an area of the United States called the Midwest. Chicago soon grew to be the largest city in the Midwest, known for its many industries.

People began moving to Chicago for jobs in

factories. African Americans moved to Chicago in large numbers after World War I. They created blues and jazz music, bringing new **culture** with them. Chicago is home to the Willis Tower, one of the tallest buildings in the Western Hemisphere. It's also home to the world's first skyscraper and one of the oldest public zoos in America.

Meatpacking was an important industry in the early years of Chicago. This is the Union Stock Yards, a famous meatpacking **district**.

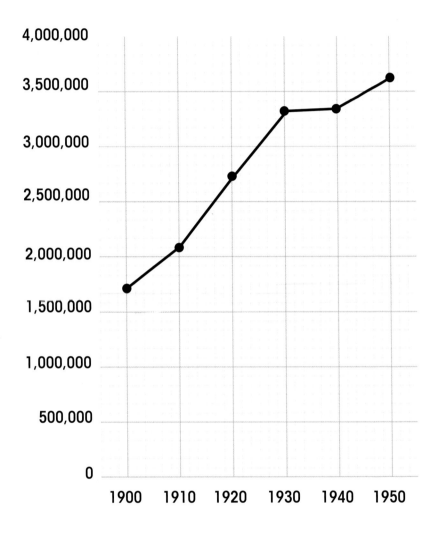

This line graph can help you see the increase in Chicago's population from 1900 to 1950.

Population Growth

You know from collecting information about the history of Chicago that the population rose quickly at first. Now, you can look at population data to check that fact. In 1900, the population of Chicago was 1,698,575. After 10 years, in 1910, the population was 2,185,283. That's a major increase in population!

In 1950, the population hit its peak with 3,620,962 people. That's almost double the population in 1900! What does this data tell you? Can you draw any inferences from it? Inferences are conclusions that are reached based on facts and reason. You can look at a line graph of the data, like the one on page 12, to help you picture the data and draw inferences.

Population Loss

During the 1950s and 1960s, the population of Chicago started to decrease. How do we know that? We have census data to support that statement!

The population went from 3,620,962 in 1950 to 3,550,404 in 1960. This may not seem like a huge drop in population, but it showed that Chicago was no longer growing. By 1990, the population was down to 2,783,726. This is a huge drop. What inferences can you draw from this drop? If you were to put this data into a line graph, what would it look like? How would it differ from the line graph you saw in the last chapter?

You might infer that more people are moving away
from Chicago than are moving to Chicago.

This is a neighborhood in a suburb of Chicago.

Chicago Today

What does Chicago's population look like today? The 2016 **population estimate** was 2,704,958. Is that more or less than the population in 1990?

You can compare today's data to data from the past. Data shows that Chicago's population is still declining, or falling. **Experts** make inferences about why population loss is happening in the city of Chicago. They've found that many people are moving to southern states, such as Arizona, Florida, and Texas, for better weather and job opportunities. Another reason people leave Chicago is because of the high cost of living. Many people move outside of the city to the suburbs for safety and cheaper housing.

Making Comparisons

You can also use population data to make comparisons between multiple cities. Chicago has the third-largest population in the United States. New York City has the highest population at an estimated 8,537,673 in 2016. Los Angeles, California, has the second-largest population at an estimated 3,976,322 in 2016.

Houston is growing because of lower costs of living and many job opportunities.

18

Chicago used to be the second-largest city, but Los Angeles's population **surpassed** that of Chicago in 1984. Today, Chicago has another competitor—Houston. Houston, Texas, has an estimated population of 2,303,482. Experts have found that while Chicago's population is dropping, Houston's population is rising. Could Houston replace Chicago as the third-largest city? You can use data to make a prediction!

Houston, Texas

Making Predictions

Experts use data to make predictions about what might happen in the future. They analyze data by looking at trends. If a population seems to be decreasing each year, then experts may predict that it will continue to decrease. If a population seems to be increasing each year, then experts may predict that it will continue to increase.

Experts also look at other factors when they make predictions. Has there been a spike in crime lately that might lead people to move from a city? Have new industries taken hold in a city that might encourage people to move there?

What will Chicago look like in the next 10 years? We can only make predictions!

What Can Data Tell You?

Looking at the population of a city is just one part of the puzzle. You can use census data to learn about demographics as well. Demographics look at the age and ethnic background of a population. For example, one place may have more young people than another. One place may have more African American residents than another. Experts can look at demographics and how they change over time to better understand what's happening in a community.

Data can help you make comparisons between two things. It can also help you to make predictions about the future. You can make your own informed inferences after looking at data!

Glossary

classify: To assign something to a category or class based on shared qualities.

culture: The beliefs and ways of life of a group of people.

determine: To conclude something with authority.

district: An area with a special feature or government.

diverse: The quality of having many different types, forms, or ideas.

ethnicity: One's classification according to common racial, national, tribal, religious, or cultural background.

expert: Someone with great knowledge about a certain subject.

industry: The businesses that provide a particular product or service.

population estimate: A count of the people in an area based on a 10-year census, while adding births, subtracting deaths, and accounting for migration each year.

surpass: To become better, greater, or stronger than.

Index